Impact Measurement and Accountability in Emergencies

The Good Enough Guide

D0746037

The Emergency Capacity Building Project

Impact Measurement and Accountability in Emergencies: The Good Enough Guide was produced as part of the Emergency Capacity Building Project. The Project was set up to address gaps in international emergency response. Its goal is to improve the speed, quality, and effectiveness with which the humanitarian community saves lives, improves the welfare, and protects the rights of women, men, and children affected by emergency.

Thanks

Funding for the Emergency Capacity Building Project comes from both the Bill & Melinda Gates Foundation and the Microsoft Corporation. Without their commitment to improving the capacity of the sector, *The Good Enough Guide* would not have been possible. We would like to thank them for their support.

Contributors

The Good Enough Guide is based on contributions from field and headquarters staff of these organisations:
- CARE International
- Catholic Relief Services
- International Rescue Committee
- Mercy Corps
- Oxfam GB
- Save the Children
- World Vision International

It is also based on contributions from staff of the Sphere Project, the Humanitarian Accountability Partnership, the Active Learning Network for Accountability and Performance in Humanitarian Action, and many other organisations. References and sources of further information are acknowledged with thanks in Section 8. There is a list of individual contributors at the back of the book.

Impact Measurement and Accountability in Emergencies

The Good Enough Guide

Emergency Capacity Building Project

First published by Oxfam GB for the Emergency Capacity Building
Project in 2007

©World Vision International, for the Emergency Capacity Building
Project 2007

ISBN 978-0-85598-594-3

A catalogue record for this publication is available from the British
Library.

This book is available from:

BEBC Distribution, PO Box 1496, Parkstone, Dorset, BH12 3YD, UK
tel: +44 (0)1202 712933; fax: +44 (0)1202 712930;
email: oxfam@bebc.co.uk

USA: Stylus Publishing LLC, PO Box 605, Herndon, VA 20172-0605, USA
tel: +1 (0)703 661 1581; fax: +1 (0)703 661 1547;
email: styluspub@aol.com

For details of local agents and representatives in other countries,
consult our website: www.oxfam.org.uk/publications
or contact Oxfam Publishing,
tel +44 (0) 1865 473727; email: publish@oxfam.org.uk

Our website contains a fully searchable database of all our titles, and
facilities for secure on-line ordering.

Published by Oxfam GB, Oxfam House, John Smith Drive, Cowley,
Oxford, OX4 2JY, UK

Printed by Information Press, Eynsham

Oxfam GB is a registered charity, no. 202 918, and is a member of Oxfam
International.

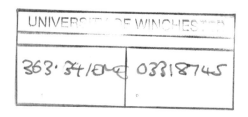

Inside the Guide

Preface:
The basic elements of accountability and impact measurement

The basic elements of accountability and impact measurement are the foundation on which *The Good Enough Guide* was developed. The basic elements listed below were drawn up by representatives of the seven agencies of the Emergency Capacity Building Project at a workshop in Nairobi in February 2006.

Basic elements of accountability

At a minimum, humanitarian project staff should:

1. Provide public information to beneficiaries and other stakeholders on their organisation, its plans, and relief assistance entitlements.

2. Conduct ongoing consultation with those assisted. This should occur as soon as possible at the beginning of a humanitarian relief operation, and continue regularly throughout it. 'Consultation' means exchange of information and views between the agency and the beneficiaries of its work. The exchange will be about:

   - The needs and aspirations of beneficiaries
   - The project plans of the agency
   - The entitlements of beneficiaries
   - Feedback and reactions from beneficiaries to the agency on its plans and expected results

3. Establish systematic feedback mechanisms that enable:

    *   Agencies to report to beneficiaries on project progress and evolution

    *   Beneficiaries to explain to agencies whether projects are meeting their needs

    *   Beneficiaries to explain to agencies the difference the project has made to their lives

4. Respond, adapt, and evolve in response to feedback received, and explain to all stakeholders the changes made and/or why change was not possible.

Basic elements of impact measurement

Impact measurement means measuring the changes in people's lives (outcomes) that result from a humanitarian project, striking a balance between qualitative and quantitative data. At a minimum, humanitarian project staff should:

1. Establish a basic description (profile) of affected people and related communities.

2. Identify desired changes, in negotiation with affected people, as soon as possible.

3. Track all project inputs and outputs against desired change.

4. Collect and document individual and community perspectives through participatory methods in order to:

    *   Increase understanding of what change they desire

    *   Help establish a baseline and track change

5. Explain methodology and limitations to all stakeholders, honestly, transparently, and objectively.

6. Use the information gathered to improve projects regularly and proactively.

What is...?

Impact measurement

In *The Good Enough Guide*, 'impact measurement' means measuring the changes taking place as the result of an emergency project. It is not always easy to do this during an emergency response. But, at its simplest, impact measurement means asking the people affected, *'What difference are we making?'*. Their view of the project and its impact is more important than anybody else's. That is why account-ability processes, which aim to make sure that those people have a say at key stages of the emergency response, are essential.

Accountability

'Accountability' is all about how an organisation balances the needs of different groups in its decision-making and activities. Most NGOs have processes in place that will meet the accountability requirements of more powerful groups such as project donors or host governments. In *The Good Enough Guide*, however, accountability means making sure that the women, men, and children affected by an emergency are involved in planning, implementing, and judging our response to their emergency too. This helps ensure that a project will have the impact they want to see.

A beneficiary

The terms 'people affected by emergencies' and 'beneficiaries' as used in *The Good Enough Guide* include all members of these groups regardless of age, disability, ethnicity, gender, HIV and AIDS status, religion, sexual orientation, or social standing unless otherwise stated.

Good enough

In this *Guide*, being 'good enough' means choosing
a simple solution rather than an elaborate one.
'Good enough' does *not* mean second best: it means
acknowledging that, in an emergency response,
adopting a quick and simple approach to impact
measurement and accountability may be the only
practical possibility. When the situation changes,
you should aim to review your chosen solution and
amend your approach accordingly.

Why and how to use The Good Enough Guide

Questions that help identify what is working and what is not often go unasked during an emergency response. They are left instead to evaluators. As a result, information that could inform decision-making and save lives is sometimes discovered only *after* a crisis is over.

One way of discovering the difference or impact a project is making is to ask the women, men, and children caught up in the emergency. For years NGOs have been promising to 'be accountable' to them: to seek their views and to put them at the heart of planning, implementing, and judging our response to their emergency.

In practice, that is a promise that has proved hard to keep. A combination of factors – including lack of know-how, time, or staff, and the situation itself – too often make impact measurement and accountability no-go areas during emergency response.

In February 2006 field staff from seven international NGOs attended a workshop in Nairobi. They took a hard look at the reality of putting impact measurement and accountability into practice on the ground during an emergency. They agreed some core ideas or Basic Elements, shown on pages 1–3. This book, the tools, and the 'good enough' approach are the result.

The Good Enough Guide is intended for field-based project officers and managers. It aims to help them make impact measurement and accountability become part of the job. It draws on the work of international NGOs and inter-agency initiatives, including

Sphere, ALNAP, HAP, and People In Aid. See page 55 for information about these initiatives.

The *Guide* does not replace the policies of individual NGOs or the common principles of inter-agency initiatives. It is not the last word on impact measurement and accountability. But, by sharing a few quick and simple approaches, *The Good Enough Guide* aims to help field-based staff ask two questions and use the answers to inform the work they do and the decisions they take:

> *What difference are we making?*
>
> *How can we involve the women, men, and children affected by an emergency in planning, implementing, and judging our response?*

How to use the Guide

You can read Sections 1–5 of the *Guide* separately or in sequence. Each Section includes links to suggested tools on impact measurement and accountability in emergencies. These tools are presented in Section 6.

Few of the tools are new. They have been adapted from the work of the Emergency Capacity Building Project and Humanitarian Accountability Partnership member agencies and from standard texts. They do not represent an exhaustive list. But the tools are collected here because field staff seldom have an opportunity to document or retrieve tools for impact measurement and accountability in the middle of an emergency response.

Remember that the 'good enough' tools are not blueprints. They are *suggested* rather than prescribed. Each can be used on its own or in conjunction with other tools. Use your own judgement, skill, and experience in deciding whether to use or adapt any tool.

Remember that field staff still need appropriate training, advice, and support.

Taking the 'good enough' approach does not mean being second best: it means using simple solutions rather than elaborate ones. A tool that is 'good enough' today can – and should – be reviewed tomorrow, in the light of needs, resources, or a security situation that has changed.

Last but not least, using the 'good enough' approach means selecting tools which are safe, quick, and easy to use in the context in which you are working. Questions to help test whether a tool is 'good enough' include:

- Can we use this tool without endangering field staff and the people affected by the emergency?
- Does it meet essential requirements in this context at this time?
- Is it realistic?
- Do we have the resources – time, staff, volunteers, and money – to use it?
- Is it useful for those applying it?
- Is it as simple as necessary?
- Have we referred to widely accepted humanitarian values, standards, and guidelines?
- Will it be 'good enough' tomorrow? When will we review our use of this tool?

Section 1 :
Involve people at every stage

Why?

It is important to involve as many stakeholders as possible in a project, including donors, local government officials, and other NGOs. But humanitarian codes, principles, standards, and mission statements stress that the women, men, and children affected by the emergency must come first. Accountability means providing them with timely and adequate information about an organisation and its proposed activities. It means making sure they have opportunities to voice their opinions, influence project design, say what results they want to see, and judge the results the project achieves. Evaluations say that involving people improves project impact. Humanitarians say accountability is also a fundamental right and value.

When?

International NGOs often assume everybody knows who they are and what they do. This is sometimes a mistake. Start providing public information about your agency as soon as situation and security allow.

Similarly, aim to provide information as often as possible about project plans and the entitlements of women, men, and children affected by the emergency (including their entitlement to relief goods and accountability). Provide information at every stage of the project cycle until you have completed your exit strategy.

How?

Use whatever means are locally available, including notice boards, meetings, newspapers, and radio broadcasts, to provide public and project information in local languages. Make sure staff, particularly new staff, are briefed about your agency and your work (**Tool 1**). Check how information reaches women as well as men during needs assessment and monitoring and that women, children, and other people affected by the emergency are not excluded. Test your accountability using **Tool 2.**

Use the 'good enough' approach and your knowledge of the local situation, resources, and security to help decide what other tools to use. Sections 2–5 give further suggestions on how to involve people throughout the response.

Suggested tools

Tool 1   How to introduce your agency: a need-to-know checklist ➤ **p30**

Tool 2   How accountable are you? Checking public information ➤ **p32**

Tool 3   How to involve people throughout the project ➤ **p34**

Tool 14 How to say goodbye ➤ **p53**

Involving people and providing information in Sri Lanka

In Ampara, soon after the 2004 Asian tsunami, we created a programme committee. We held a big public meeting, and asked people to identify 15 volunteers to support the work. We did the analysis with these volunteers.

For transparency, we put up the beneficiaries' list on a public notice board with the criteria used to select them. We gave the community one week to look at the list and raise complaints. In Batticaloa, we did the same thing.
We are bringing out a 4-page leaflet about our work so people will know about us.

Source: Cherian Mathew, Oxfam GB Sri Lanka

Section 2:
Profile the people affected by the emergency

Why?

Establish a basic profile of the population to help decide who is most in need of your assistance. Women and men will be affected differently by the emergency. Some people will be at greater risk than others, because of their age, disability, ethnicity, social status, or religion.

Basic information about the population is essential to help you begin making decisions about your response. Agencies that respond without starting to assess who is affected and in what way may offer assistance which is unnecessary, inappropriate, or fails to reach the most vulnerable.

When?

Humanitarian agencies need to act quickly when lives are in imminent danger. Do not wait until you have perfect information about the people affected. But do start building a profile of those affected as early as possible during the needs-assessment phase. Continue to update your information and add to it as the situation changes and when you find out more.

How?

Every emergency is different. Slow-onset disasters
may allow more time for assessment. But in conflict
or sudden-onset emergencies, collecting information
can be difficult and dangerous for field staff and beneficiaries. That makes it very important for staff to
know what secondary information is already available.
Secondary information can come from:

- Your local field staff
- Your agency's files
- Another organisation, for example, the govern-
  ment, the United Nations, a local or international
  NGO

Government and United Nations agencies, for example,
are likely to hold statistical data on the area affected
by the emergency.

Nevertheless, in most emergencies it is possible to
involve at least some beneficiaries directly before
your response starts. Profiling can be repeated when
time allows and access is easier.

Assessment teams should include both women and
men: an all-male team will find it difficult to assess
female vulnerability. The team should talk to women
as well as men and assess the needs of other groups at
additional risk such as children (**Tool 8**). Staff should
try to cross-check the information they receive when-
ever possible, in order to test its accuracy.

Aim to co-ordinate assistance with local and international NGOs where possible: conduct joint assessments,
capitalise on local resources, share information and
decisions, and/or identify gaps.

Suggested tools

Involving people affected by an emergency before humanitarian response starts

During sudden crises there is an imperative to act quickly. But it is always possible to speak to some affected people. Given time constraints, only a few interviews will be possible, so interviewees must be carefully selected.

The first step is to identify areas most affected, using secondary information and key informants. Secondly, the most vulnerable groups are selected through rapid, on-the-spot consultation with different stakeholders. Finally, random sampling is used to select individual and group informants.

Each of these three steps can be done in less than an hour, though with more time the accuracy of the process will be improved.

Agencies should not delay the initial deployment of resources until perfect information is received. But they should adjust activities as the quality of information improves. Assessment and implementation must run in parallel.

Source: IFRC (2005) *World Disasters Report 2005*.

Section 3:
Identify the changes people want to see

Why?

People affected by an emergency are the best judges of their own interests. The changes they want to see are important indicators of the difference a project is likely to make and the impact it will have. When beneficiaries are enabled to identify those changes and contribute to decision-making, project impact is likely to be greater. Conversely, when people are not involved, a response can miss its mark, leave out vulnerable groups, waste money, and add to suffering.

People who have been involved in designing a project are more likely to feel it is theirs and to take responsibility for it. That is particularly important when NGOs supply equipment, for example water pumps and latrines, that requires long-term maintenance by the community.

When?

Pressure from media, donors, and governments can be overwhelming at the start of a response. It can push agencies into making promises and commitments they may be unable to keep. But ask people affected as soon as possible how *they* feel and what *they* want to see happen as a result of the project. It is their home, their family, and their world that have been turned upside down.

Consultation does not mean a one-off meeting after all the big decisions have been made by others. It means communicating timely and relevant information

to help people make decisions, negotiating throughout the project cycle, and being open and realistic
about what your agency can and can't do.

How?

Use more than one method of consulting people if
possible: for example, a village meeting (**Tool 3**) plus
focus group (**Tool 6**), in order to reach different people.
Hold separate discussions to find out what particular
groups within the community want. Don't assume
that traditional figures of authority speak on behalf of
women, children, older people, or other potentially
vulnerable or marginalised groups.

Use consultation to start developing quantitative and
qualitative indicators that are important for the community (**Tool 10**). Keep a basic written record of your
discussions, the needs identified, and the indicators
set (even if donors don't ask you to). Use these records
to help measure change and impact, document
important lessons learned, and inform project staff
and project activities (**Tool 11**).

Suggested tools

Tool 3   How to involve people throughout the project ➤ **p34**

Tool 5   How to conduct an individual interview ➤ **p38**

Tool 6   How to conduct a focus group ➤ **p40**

Tool 10   How to start using indicators ➤ **p45**

Tool 11   How to hold a lessons-learned meeting ➤ **p48**

Consult people about what *they* want to see as soon as possible

Governments, NGOs, and private contractors moved fast to start providing temporary houses for homeless families after the 2004 tsunamis. But they rarely involved affected families in the planning discussions. In the worst cases, some houses were poorly designed, proved impossible to live in, and had to be demolished.

In a pilot scheme in Sri Lanka, Oxfam held planning work-shops with homeless women and men. Oxfam used global standards and indicators developed by the Sphere Project. Its field staff also agreed local house size, design, materials, and construction in discussions with affected families before building began.

Source: Ivan Scott, Oxfam GB

Section 4:
Track changes and make feedback a two-way process

Why?

Keep track of goods and services delivered in order to find out how well project activities are running. But also invite feedback, including complaints, from people affected by the emergency, to see if the project is achieving the changes they want to see. Make feedback a two-way process. Report to beneficiaries on progress against indicators and about the issues they raise.

Tracking changes and establishing two-way feedback are essential for:

- Making decisions and improvements
- Identifying gaps, new needs, and possible problems
- Giving staff support and a response to their work
- Making sure money is well-spent
- Keeping the community and other stakeholders informed and involved
- Demonstrating accountability

Feedback can be positive or negative, but complaints mean that things may have gone wrong. A complaints and response mechanism is necessary for impact, accountability, and learning. It is essential for identifying any corruption, abuse, or exploitation.

When?

Tracking, feedback, and reporting to people affected by the emergency should take place as often as possible throughout the project. It is particularly important when field staff turnover is high: it helps maintain continuity and a common understanding of project focus. A complaints and response system should be in place as soon as possible at the start of the project (**Tool 12**).

How?

Use project records to help prepare questions that track progress and changes against indicators already set. If no indicators have been developed with the community, use feedback as an opportunity to do so.

Collect and record both individual and community views of the project. Make sure that different groups within the community are able to give feedback in separate groups if necessary. Co-ordinate with other local and international NGOs where possible, sharing information or inviting them to take part in your lessons-learned meetings (**Tool 11**).

Don't collect more information than you can analyse and use. Report as often as you can to committees and groups affected and to other significant stakeholders. Use photos, film, and displays if possible to show changes that have taken place since the project started. What is progress against the indicators set? What are you learning from feedback and complaints?

If your report is based on limited information, perhaps from a single village or focus group, be transparent and explain why this is so. Are there any changes or delays to the project? Explain the reasons. After your report, give people an opportunity to talk back.

Suggested tools

Tracking beneficiary feedback in Darfur

Medair staff asked 800 patients at ten clinics in west Darfur to give them feedback about the services provided.

After a clinic visit, each patient put a disc with a smiley or not-so-smiley face into one of three different containers. The disc indicated level of satisfaction with 1) waiting time, 2) staff conduct, and 3) quality of information about medicines prescribed.

By counting the smiles and frowns, staff could quickly gauge levels of satisfaction and turn these into percentages. The percentages could act as quantitative indicators to check change in satisfaction levels in the future.

Source: Rebekka Meissner, Zachariah Ahmed Adam, and Robert Schofield, Medair

Section 5:
Use feedback to improve project impact

Why?

Tracking, feedback, and reporting help field teams learn what is working and what is not working during the project. Mistakes can have serious consequences for people affected by an emergency. Sharing lessons and taking action in the course of the project means good practice can be replicated and not-so-good practice rectified as soon as possible.

When?

Analyse, summarise, and feed the information from tracking and beneficiary feedback into planning meetings as soon as possible. If information from this process is not used, collecting it is a waste of time and resources for staff and beneficiaries.

Take urgent action before scheduled planning meetings if necessary, for example if monitoring discloses any of the following: evidence of poor quality, risk to staff or beneficiaries, or allegations of corruption or sexual abuse. Share success and credit at the end of the project or when handing it over to the community.

How?

Do use the information collected through feedback or when tracking progress against indicators to inform project decisions and changes. **Tool 12** and the box on page 27 are evidence of how monitoring and complaints mechanisms can identify gaps and improve project impact and coverage.

Think about the frequently asked questions or complaints you have received: can you include the answers in need-to-know lists for field staff (**Tool 1**) or information sheets for people affected by the emergency?

Consider inviting beneficiaries to a lessons-learned meeting. Keep a written record of discussions that lead to significant project changes and the reasons for making them. Share progress reports with beneficiaries (**Tool 13**). Don't forget to say goodbye at the end of the project. Share success, lessons learned, and credit with the community. Mark the end of the project with appropriate formality, courtesy, and celebration (**Tool 14**).

Suggested tools

Tool 1   How to introduce your agency: a need-to-know checklist ➤ **p30**

Tool 11   How to hold a lessons-learned meeting ➤ **p48**

Tool 12   How to set up a complaints and response mechanism ➤ **p49**

Tool 13   How to give a verbal report ➤ **p52**

Tool 14   How to say goodbye ➤ **p53**

Using feedback from children to try to improve impact

The C-SAFE project in Southern Africa involves CARE, Catholic Relief Services, World Vision, and Adventist Development & Relief Agency International (ADRA). Its 'Listening to Children' exercise in Zimbabwe was set up to monitor a school feeding programme and understand food insecurity from the children's perspective.

Staff of C-SAFE used individual interviews and focus groups. Five schools from each district in Zimbabwe were selected. Three children from each class were interviewed every month. There were separate focus groups for the oldest girls and boys. In all, 5000 children were interviewed.

Findings went beyond quantitative indicators about the children (age, height, weight), important as these are. C-SAFE found that many of the interviewees' classmates could not pay the small fee charged by schools to cover the cost of preparing the food. In some cases children had been barred from eating the food and in other cases they had been prevented from attending school.

While the fees were necessary for some schools, analysis revealed that fees were doing more harm than good. C-SAFE therefore consulted local government officials and head teachers on how to remove the fees or soften the requirements, and at the same time raised extra funds for the neediest schools.

Source: Consortium for Southern Africa Food Security Emergency, September 2005

Section 6:
Tools

List of tools

Using the 'good enough' tools

Remember: using the 'good enough' approach means selecting tools which are essential, safe, quick, and easy to use in the situation in which you are working. The tools are not blueprints. They are suggested not prescribed. These are not the only tools. Use your own experience and judgement in deciding whether to use a particular tool, when to use it, and how to adapt it for the time and place you are working in.

Questions that can help you test whether a tool is 'good enough' include:

- Can we use this tool without endangering field staff and the people affected by the emergency?
- Does it meet essential requirements in this context at this time?
- Is it realistic?
- Do we have the resources – time, staff, volunteers, and money – to use it?
- Is it useful for those applying it?
- Is it as simple as necessary?
- Have we referred to widely accepted humanitarian values, standards, and guidelines?
- Will it be 'good enough' tomorrow? When will we review our use of this tool?

Tool 1:
How to introduce your agency:
a need-to-know checklist

This checklist can be used to help make sure field staff
know the answers to questions they are likely to be asked
by beneficiaries, government officials, and others.
You can use it at the start of a project or in conjunction with
Tool 11 to brief new staff.

Who are we?

1. What is an NGO?
2. What is our mandate?
3. Why is our agency here?
4. Where do we get the money?

Our aim

5. What can we do for people affected by the emergency
   in relation to:
   a) Water and sanitation
   b) Shelter
   c) Livelihoods
   d) Public health promotion
   e) Other kinds of project

6. Why do we do this rather than other things?

The project and the community

7. What is our project area?
8. Who decided?
9. Who was involved in deciding project activities?
10. What is the plan for the whole project?
11. How long will it last?
12. Who are the beneficiaries?
13. Why were some people chosen and not others?
14. Who was involved in deciding who the beneficiaries
    should be?

15. How does the project work? How are beneficiaries involved?
16. What will beneficiaries contribute?
17. What will we contribute?
18. What do the materials cost us?
19. What is the progress this month? What is the plan for next month?
20. What are the main challenges for technical staff this month?
21. What are technical staff doing to address these challenges?
22. What exactly will beneficiaries receive?
23. When will they receive it?

Dealing with problems or complaints (see also Tool 13)

24. If something goes wrong with the project what can people do?
25. If there is a problem with a community leader or community member working with us, what can people do?
26. If there is a problem with one of our staff (corruption, fraud, bad behaviour), what can people do?

Other organisations and the government

27. Which other NGOs are working in the project location?
28. What do they do?
29. What government assistance is available? How do people access it?
30. What other problems are people having? (For example, being displaced, no access to land, not being able to meet government officials to resolve problems.)

From T. Gorgonio and A. Miller (2005) 'Need To Know List', Oxfam GB (internal, adapted).

Tool 2:
How accountable are you?
Checking public information

This tool can help you check whether you are providing people affected by the emergency with basic information about your agency and the project. By asking people what information they have received, you can check how they see you and whether you are providing the information they need at the right time in the right way.

This tool can be used at different stages during the project: at the start to help you explain who you are and what your agency can do (see also **Tool 1**); after significant changes, for example, if the level of food ration is cut; and at the end of a project as part of your exit strategy.

For field team members

Have you provided the checklist information (opposite) to beneficiaries and their representatives in an accessible way?

For people affected by an emergency

Have you received the checklist information (opposite) from project staff?

Checklist

Basic information	Yes	No
1 Background information about the NGO		
2 Details of the current project		
3 Project contact information		
Reports on project implementation		
4 Regular reports on project performance		
5 Regular financial reports		
6 Information about significant project changes		
Opportunities for involvement		
7 Dates and locations of key participation events		
8 Specific contact details for making comments or suggestions		
9 Details of how to make complaints about the NGO's activities		

From A. Jacobs (2005) 'Accountability to Beneficiaries: A Practical Checklist', draft, Mango for Oxfam GB (adapted).

Tool 3:
How to involve people throughout the project

This tool suggests ways of informing, consulting, involving, and reporting to people affected by an emergency at every stage of the project. It was originally developed for use in villages in Aceh. It can be adapted for other sites too.

Before assessment

- Determine and clearly state the objectives of the assessment
- If you can, inform the local community and local authorities well before the assessment takes place
- Include both women and men in the project team
- Make a list of vulnerable groups to be identified during the assessment
- Check what other NGOs have done in that community and get a copy of their reports

During assessment

- Introduce team members and their roles
- Explain the timeframe for assessment
- Invite representatives of local people to participate
- Create space for individuals or groups to speak openly
- Hold separate discussions and interviews with different groups, for example: local officials, community groups, men, women, local staff
- Ask these groups for their opinions on needs and priorities. Inform them about any decisions taken.

  Note: If it is not possible to consult all groups within the community at one time, state clearly which groups have been omitted on this occasion and return to meet them as soon as possible. Write up your findings and describe your methodology and its limitations. Use the analysis for future decision-making.

During project design

- Give local authorities and community, including the village committee and representatives of affected groups, the findings of the assessment

- Invite representatives of local people to participate in project design
- Explain to people their rights as disaster-affected people
- Enable the village committee to take part in project budgeting
- Check the project design with different groups of beneficiaries
- Design a complaints and response mechanism

During project implementation

- Invite local community, village committee, and local authorities to take part in developing criteria for selection of beneficiaries
- Announce the criteria and display them in a public place
- Invite the local community and village committee to participate in selecting beneficiaries
- Announce the beneficiaries and post the list in a public place
- Announce the complaints and response mechanisms and forum for beneficiaries to raise complaints

During distribution

- If recruiting additional staff for distribution, advertise openly, e.g. in newspaper
- Form a distribution committee comprising the village committee, government official(s), and NGO staff
- Consider how distribution will include the most vulnerable, such as disabled people, elderly people, and other poor or marginalised groups
- Give the local authority and local community a date and location for distribution in advance where safety allows
- List items for distribution and their cost and display this list in advance in a public place
- In order to include people living a long way from the village or distribution point, consider giving them transport costs
- In order to include vulnerable people, such as pregnant women, for example, distribute to them first
- Ensure people know how to register complaints

During monitoring

- Invite the village committee to take part in the monitoring process
- Share findings with the village committee and community

From S. Phoeuk (2005) 'Practical Guidelines on Humanitarian Accountability', Oxfam GB Cambodia (internal, adapted).

Tool 4:

How to profile the affected community and assess initial needs

This tool can help you profile an affected community.
It can be used in conjunction with **Tool 5** and **Tool 6** and repeated as the situation changes.

Suggested questions

1. What is the background of the affected group(s)? Are they from an urban or rural background?

2. What is the approximate number of people affected and their demographic characteristics? (Include a breakdown of the population by sex, and children under five. Include numbers of 5–14-year-olds, pregnant and lactating women, and those aged 60 and over, if data are available.)

3. Who are the marginalised/separated people in this population group (for example, female-headed households, unaccompanied children, disabled, sick, elderly, ethnic minorities, etc.). Do they have specific needs? How have they been affected by the current crisis?

4. Are there particular family, ethnic, religious, or other groupings among the affected people? Are any groups particularly hard to access?

5. Who are the key people to contact/consult? Are there any community members or elders leading the people affected by the emergency? Are there organisations with local expertise (for example, churches, mosques, or local NGOs) that can be part of decision-making?

6. What are the biggest risks, in terms of health and protection against violence, faced by the various groups of people affected by this emergency and what agency is addressing them?

How have women been affected?
Do they have specific needs?

'In the early stages in Gujarat our distribution teams were almost exclusively male. The SPHERE guidelines prompted us to send an all-female survey team into earthquake-affected communities to talk to women. As a result, we developed a hygiene kit for women and got funding for 23,000 kits.'

'The immediate relief operations in Sri Lanka were largely gender-blind. Few organisations considered providing women with sanitary needs, underwear or culturally appropriate clothing. The needs of pregnant or breastfeeding mothers were not sufficiently catered for.'

Source: Srodecki (2001); IFRC (2005)

From Oxfam (no date) 'Background Information: Checklist for Rapid Assessments In Emergencies'(adapted); IFRC (2000) *Disaster Preparedness Training Manual* (adapted); IFRC (2005) *World Disasters Report 2005* (adapted); J. Srodecki (2001) 'World Vision use of Sphere standards in a large scale emergency: a case study of the spring 2001 Gujarat response', World Vision (internal, adapted).

Tool 5:
How to conduct an individual interview

Individual interviews can be used during assessments or surveys. An individual interview can mean a ten-minute conversation during an informal visit or a longer and more structured discussion, using a series of questions on a particular topic. Whatever the case, focus on essential information and build your interview around current concerns, for example, profiling and needs assessment, tracking changes, or seeking feedback.

Aim to interview people at times that are safe and convenient for both staff and interviewees. The time your interviewee has available should determine how long your interview lasts. Make sure that people understand why you wish to talk to them and what you will do with the information they share. Never use people's names when using information without their express permission or that of their guardian.

Start with questions that are factual and relatively straightforward to answer. Move on to more sensitive issues, if necessary, only when the person you are interviewing is more at ease.

Make sure people know that you value their time and participation. Don't end the interview too abruptly. Take responsibility for the effect on your interviewee if sensitive issues are discussed.

Record, store, and use information safely.

Some 'Do's' for interviews

- Do try to make sure you have a good translator.
- Do locate elders/leaders first, explain who you are and what you are doing, and ask their permission to interview.
- Do ask individuals' permission to interview them; for example, 'Is it OK if I ask you a few questions about the conditions here?' Thank them afterwards.
- Do try to prioritise discussions with women and children, and other people likely to be experiencing particular difficulty.
- Do try and interview at least three families in each location in order to cross-check the information you are receiving.
- Do make sure that you include people at the edge of a camp or site where you may find the poorest families living, quite literally, on the margins.
- Do avoid large crowds following you around if possible, since this is likely to intimidate interviewees and interviewers.

Source: Schofield (2003)

From S. Burns and S. Cupitt (2003) 'Managing outcomes: a guide for homelessness organisations', Charities Evaluation Services (adapted); R. Schofield, Medair (internal, adapted).

Tool 6:
How to conduct a focus group

If possible, conduct a few focus groups and compare the information you are collecting from these and other sources.

What is a focus group?

Six to twelve people are invited to discuss specific topics in detail.

The focus group can bring together people who have something in common. They may share a particular problem, or be unable to speak up at larger meetings (for example, younger people, women, or minority groups), or are people only peripherally involved in the community, such as nomads. It is best not to have leaders or people in authority present – interview them separately.

Why only six to twelve people?

In a larger group:

- Speaking time will be restricted and dominant people will speak most
- The facilitator will have to play more of a controlling role
- Some members of the group will become frustrated if they cannot speak
- Participants will start talking to one other rather than to the group as a whole
- The group may stop focusing and start talking about something else

What do you need?

- An experienced facilitator: a native speaker who can lead, draw out the people who are not talking, and stop others from talking too much
- Time to prepare open-ended questions and select focus-group members
- One, sometimes two, people to note in writing what is said
- A common language
- A quiet place where the group will not be overheard or interrupted
- To sit in a circle and be comfortable

- Shared understanding and agreement about the purpose of the discussion
- Ground rules, for example: everyone has a right to speak; no one has the right answer; please don't interrupt
- Permission from the group to take notes (or maybe use a tape recorder)
- About one to one-and-a-half hours and some refreshments

What happens?

- The facilitator makes sure everyone has a chance to speak and that the discussion stays focused
- The note-taker writes notes
- At the end of the session, the facilitator gives a brief summing up of what has been said in case someone has something to add
- The facilitator checks that the written record has captured the main points and reflected the level of participants' involvement in the discussion.

From V. M. Walden (no date) 'Focus group discussion', Oxfam (internal. adapted); L. Gosling and M. Edwards (2003) *Toolkits: a practical guide to planning, monitoring, evaluation and impact measurement*, Save the Children (adapted); USAID (1996) *Performance Monitoring and Evaluation TIPS No. 10*, USAID Centre for Development Information and Evaluation (adapted).

Tool 7:
How to decide whether to do a survey

Surveys can be used to collect information from large numbers of people before, during, or after a project. Surveys are useful tools but can be complex and resource-intensive in practice. Before deciding if you are ready to conduct a survey, think about some of the advantages and disadvantages.

Surveys: some advantages and disadvantages

Advantages	Disadvantages
A survey can provide specific information about a lot of people in a short time.	Only a short time can be spent with each person so the information you receive about them may be limited.
	You will also need time to analyse and use all the information collected.
Information from some of the people can be used to make plans for all the population.	The people selected may be easy to get to or willing to co-operate but not necessarily representative of the population.
The methods and forms used to collect information must be standardised so that results can be reliably compared (for example, see **Tool 8**).	These methods may produce superficial information. Interviewees may give the answers they think you want to hear.
A survey requires careful consideration beforehand in order to determine what information can be obtained, from whom, how, and when.	Time may be scarce. If people's way of life is not fully understood then the information they provide may prove misleading.
A large amount of information can be obtained cheaply if unpaid or volunteer staff are used.	A large-scale survey is often difficult to supervise because of staff costs and distances to be covered.

Tool 8:
How to assess child-protection needs

This basic checklist can be used in the different areas in which you work or plan to work. It can be further adapted to assess protection needs for other vulnerable groups too. See pages 59–62 for other resources and checklists.

1. Are there any reported cases of children:
   • killed in this disaster
   • injured
   • missing?

2. Are there groups of children without access to:
   • food
   • water
   • shelter
   • health care
   • education?

3. Have these cases been reported? To which organisation?

4. Are there any reported cases of
   • separated children
   • families with missing children
   • children sent away to safe places?

5. Have families generally moved as a group?

6. Are there groups of children living together without adults? Do they include children less than five years of age?

7. Are there individual adults who have assumed care responsibility for a large group of children?

8. List any organisations taking care of separated children.

9. Are there other serious protection and care concerns for girls not already identified above?

10. Are there other serious protection and care concerns for boys not already identified above?

11. Which organisations are working on child-protection issues in the area?

From World Vision (no date) 'Rapid child protection assessment form in situations of natural disasters', (internal, adapted).

Tool 9:
How to observe

In some situations, informal observation may be all you can do and 'good enough' when making an assessment or tracking changes.

'I look to see if people are moving into houses. I ask if they feel safe. Are they smiling? Are they happy? I look to see if children are going back to school.' (John Watt)

Observing people:
some tips and possible problems

Tips	Possible problems
Explain why you want to observe people at the site, and how the information you collect will be used. Request permission from the people living there.	Observing people may affect their normal behaviour and routines.
Invite people living there to observe the site with you.	If an observer knows the people being observed well, this may make it hard for him/her to be unbiased.
Give observers brief training and support. Agree the information you want to collect through observation.	Involving many observers can result in many different opinions and interpretations.
Afterwards, compare notes and pool observations as soon as you can. Record your findings in writing and use them.	Findings that are not recorded immediately will be less reliable.

From *Partners in Evaluation: Evaluating Development and Community Programmes with Participants*, © Marie-Thérèse Feuerstein 1986. Reproduced by permission of Macmillan Publishers Ltd.

Tool 10:
How to start using indicators

Your agency may have its own approach to indicators. If not, this introduction can help you start to develop 'good enough' indicators with people affected by an emergency.

Indicators are numbers or statements that help measure, simplify, and communicate changes and impact.

Quantitative indicators use numbers, qualitative indicators use words or pictures. Both types of indicator are necessary. For example, a quantitative indicator may tell you the number of children receiving rations: a qualitative indicator can tell you how satisfied they are with the food.

Use the 'good enough' approach when thinking about indicators:

• Find out if the project already has some indicators

• Don't develop too many new ones: use as few as possible

• Try to have a balance of quantitative and qualitative indicators

• Collect only the information you need most

• Check that a preferred indicator really will measure the change desired

• After using your indicators to track changes, analyse and use this information in decision-making

Sphere indicators

The 'good enough' approach recognises the need to refer to widely accepted standards. Sphere provides the best-known indicators of humanitarian impact. They create a 'common language' and enable comparison between projects.

Sphere acknowledges that indicators may be modified in certain contexts. In the case below an agency explains why it could not deliver the recommended 7–15 litres of water per person per day. When indicators cannot be met, it is important to be transparent, to record reasons during assessment and impact monitoring and, if possible, to advocate so that indicators can be met.

Ethiopia project

In a drought project in Ethiopia in 2000 we delivered water to over 400,000 people. We delivered approximately 5 litres per person per day instead of the recommended 15 litres. That was beyond donor and logistical capacities. We clearly stated that we were delivering water only for consumption and cooking.

Indicators of change

Wherever possible, involve women, men, and children affected by the emergency in deciding the changes they want to see. Ask community members at a meeting, workshop, or in individual discussion about what they hope to see when the project has been completed. Hold separate meetings for women and for other groups.

Ask people affected about what will happen if the project is a success. 'Imagine the project is finished. How will people benefit? How will it affect your life? What will you see happening?' People's response to these questions helps give you the indicators you need to track progress and change.

Indicators of change developed by a community:
- may or may not be compatible with other indicators
- may seem illogical to outsiders
- may not be applicable in other emergencies or other communities
- may not be time-bound
- may not enable comparison between projects

However, they are a way of making sure project staff look through the eyes of beneficiaries, enable people to express their views, and take into account their experience and wishes.

Sudan project

In a water project in south Sudan, project staff gauged success using a Sphere indicator that measured the distance of the water point from the community.

But in the same project the community measured success by counting the number of girls going to school. When the water point was nearer the community, the girls took their buckets to school and picked up the water on the way home.

How did people feel about the changes in their community as a result of the water supply close by and the fact that girls could go to school? An example of how to measure satisfaction is shown in the box on page 23.

From V. M. Walden (2005) 'Community Indicators', Oxfam (internal); L. Bishop (2002) 'First steps in Monitoring and Evaluation', Charities Evaluation Services; interview with Margarita Clark, Save the Children.

Tool 11:
How to hold a lessons-learned meeting

Purpose

- For project staff to meet and to share project information
- To build agreement on the activities you are carrying out
- To build agreement on the changes you aim to make
- To document key information and decisions and act on them

You will need

- Your accountability adviser, if you have one
- One person to act as facilitator
- Another person to record in writing key findings, comments, and decisions

Questions for project staff

1. Which people are you working with?
2. Which of these people are particularly vulnerable?
3. Who have you spoken to since the last meeting?
4. What have you learnt from them?
5. Who have you cross-referenced findings with?
6. How do findings compare with your meeting records and/or baseline data?
7. What needs are beneficiaries prioritising?
8. How does this relate to your current activities?
9. What is working well?
10. What is not working well?
11. What results are/should you aim to achieve and how?
12. What do you need to do to improve impact?

When meetings are held regularly, with key findings, comments, decisions, and dates noted, this can help you update project information and measure project impact. It is particularly important to try to do this during the early stages when you are busy responding, when staff turnover may be high, and when teams have little time to set up systems.

From written communication with Pauline Wilson and staff at
World Vision International (adapted).

Tool 12:

How to set up a complaints and response mechanism

Feedback can be positive or negative: complaints mean that things may have gone wrong. Receiving complaints and responding to them is central to accountability, impact, and learning.

Information

Tell people how to complain and that it is their right to do so.

- Use staff and notice boards to give information about complaints processes
- Be clear about the types of complaint you can and can't deal with
- Know your agency's procedures on abuse or exploitation of beneficiaries
- Explain details of the appeals process

Accessibility

Make access to the complaints process as easy and safe as possible. Consider:

- How will beneficiaries in remote locations be able to make complaints?
- Can complaints be received verbally or only in writing?
- Is it possible to file a complaint on behalf of somebody else (owing to their illiteracy, fears for their personal safety, inability to travel, etc.)?

Procedures

Describe how complaints will be handled.

- Develop a standard complaints form
- Give the complainant a receipt, preferably a copy of their signed form
- Enable an investigation to be tracked and keep statistics on complaints and responses
- Keep complaint files confidential. Ensure discussion about the complaint cannot be traced back to the individual complainant
- Know your agency's procedures for dealing with complaints against staff

Response

Give beneficiaries a response to their complaint.

* Make sure each complainant receives a response and appropriate action
* Be consistent: ensure similar complaints receive a similar response
* Maintain oversight of complaints processes and have an appeals process

Learning

Learning from complaints and mistakes.

* Collect statistics and track any trends
* Feed learning into decision-making and project activities

A complaints and response mechanism in action

Medair responded to the Kashmir earthquake in October 2005 with emergency shelter and non-food items. The team soon realised it needed a mechanism to address constant queries and complaints. One hour a day was dedicated to dealing with complaints at the main project base. This was the only time Medair would receive complaints.

A complainant could speak to the Administrator or Office Manager. If possible, complaints were resolved informally. Otherwise, office staff completed a complaints form and passed this to an Assessment Team in the field. Complaints about staff members were investigated by the Project Manager at each base.

Most complaints came from earthquake survivors who had not received a shelter. They also came from people outside Medair's own project area. In those cases Medair lobbied the responsible agency. Sometimes, if nothing happened, Medair provided help itself. If a complaint investigated by an Assessment Team was upheld, the beneficiary received assistance, depending on Medair's resources.

A spreadsheet recorded the numbers of complaints from each village, and how many complaints had been dealt with. This enabled project staff to assess progress and to integrate complaints into project planning.

By the end of the emergency phase, Medair had dealt with approximately 1600 complaints, 70 per cent of all those it had received. Not all complaints could be investigated because by March 2006 Medair had used up its project funds. Checking more households would raise false expectations. Also, five months after the earthquake, most homes had been rehabilitated. Of the complaints investigated 18 per cent were upheld. Complaints about staff led to dismissal for three who had given preferential treatment to their tribal or family members.

The complaints mechanism saved Medair teams significant time in field and office and in identifying gaps in coverage. By using this mechanism Medair helped 290 families whose needs would otherwise have been overlooked.

Medair was new to Pakistan and the complaints and response mechanism helped compensate for limited local knowledge. By the end of the project, communities would contact Medair about any discrepancy they saw in its distributions, confident that the agency would take appropriate action.

From written communication with Robert Schofield and John Primrose, Medair (adapted).

Tool 13:
How to give a verbal report

Even when people affected by the emergency have participated throughout the project, some people will know more about it than others. Here are some tips for giving a verbal report about the project to the community in general.

Keep it short

Don't hide information but aim to help people remember the main points about what has happened.

Think what people need to know

Prepare a verbal presentation that suits people's needs.

Emphasise key points

If you can, use posters, quotes, photos, slides, tables, and charts.

Encourage participation

A Question & Answer session, a panel, or a short play can help.

Encourage people to say what they think

People may have conflicting views of the project and the changes it is making. Think ahead about how you will deal with these different views.

Listen and be tactful

Try to maintain a good atmosphere and good relationships between people, especially if they express different views. Try to end the discussion on a positive note.

From *Partners in Evaluation: Evaluating Development and Community Programmes with Participants*, © Marie-Thérèse Feuerstein 1986. Reproduced by permission of Macmillan Publishers Ltd.

Tool 14:
How to say goodbye

This tool can help ensure that your agency's departure at the end of the project is smooth and transparent. The people who have been involved in your project, including beneficiaries, staff, and local partner agencies and authorities, should know what is happening and why.

Define in detail communication needs and activities. These may include:

1. Writing a letter to staff followed by group and individual meetings
2. Writing an official letter about project closure for regional, district, and village leaders, including elders and informal leaders

   Follow letters with face-to-face briefings

   Put a copy of the letter to village leaders on information boards
3. Using a Question & Answer sheet to guide staff when communicating with beneficiaries about end of project
4. Planning for the conduct of exit meetings with communities
5. Reporting on project achievements and learning
6. Writing a letter to other NGOs and partners

   Follow with face-to-face briefings and meetings
7. Holding focus groups and/or house-to-house visits to reach women and vulnerable groups who may be unable to attend formal meetings
8. Using posters and leaflets, including formats appropriate for less literate people
9. Inviting feedback/comments on project activities
10. Collecting stories about successful work and positive community interaction

    Give these back to the community; for example have a photo exhibition during handover
11. Supporting appropriate cultural activities or celebration when projects are handed over to the community
12. Evaluating exit communication activities and recording lessons learned

From T. Gorgonio (2006) 'Notes on Accountable Exit from Communities when Programmes Close', Oxfam GB Philippines (internal, adapted).

Section 7:
Other accountability initiatives

The Good Enough Guide draws on the work of numerous organisations, including aid-sector initiatives ALNAP, HAP International, People In Aid, and Sphere. For more information see the links below.

ALNAP

ALNAP was established in 1997 following a multi-agency evaluation of response to the Rwanda genocide. ALNAP members include organisations and experts from across the humanitarian sector, including donor, NGO, Red Cross/Red Crescent, UN, and independent/academic organisations. ALNAP is dedicated to improving the quality and accountability of humanitarian action by sharing lessons, identifying common problems and, where appropriate, building consensus on approaches. **www.alnap.org**

HAP International

The Humanitarian Accountability Partnership was founded in 2003 by a group of humanitarian agencies committed to making their work more accountable to disaster survivors. HAP membership requires a formal commitment to uphold HAP's Principles of Accountability developed through five years of action research and field trials. The HAP Accountability and Quality Management Standard comprises a set of auditable benchmarks that assure accountability to beneficiaries. HAP's Manual of Accountability includes sections of *The Good Enough Guide*. **www.hapinternational.org**

People In Aid

Established in 1995, People In Aid is a global network of development and humanitarian assistance agencies. It helps organisations enhance the impact their projects make through better management and support of staff and volunteers. The People In Aid Code of Good Practice comprises seven principles defined by indicators. Commitment to the Code can be verified at regular intervals by an external social auditor. Since 2001 compliance with the Code has been recognised through the award of People In Aid quality marks.

www.peopleinaid.org

Sphere

Sphere was launched in 1997 by a group of humanitarian NGOs and the Red Cross/Red Crescent Movement. It has developed a handbook which includes a Humanitarian Charter, Standards for four sectors (Water/Sanitation and Hygiene Promotion; Food Security; Nutrition and Food Aid; Settlement and Non-Food Items and Health Services) plus Standards common to all sectors. The Charter and Standards contribute to an operational framework for accountability in disaster assistance. The handbook is revised regularly in consultation with users. The most recent revision was published in 2004 and the next is due in 2009.

www.sphereproject.org

Section 8:
Sources, further information, and abbreviations

The references given in this section have been organised according to the Section of the *Guide* to which they relate. 'Sources' include all documentation from which material has been drawn, and 'Further information' points the reader to further useful resources on particular topics. All Internet addresses given were last accessed in December 2006.

Involve people at every stage (Section 1)

Sources:

Bhattacharjee, A., Rawal, V., Fautin, C., Moore, J.-L., Kalonge, S. and Walden, V. (2005) 'Multi-Agency Evaluation of Tsunami Response: India and Sri Lanka Evaluation', CARE International, Oxfam GB, and World Vision International, available at: http://www.ecb project.org/publications/ECB2/Multi-Agency%20 Evaluation%20-%20India%20and%20Sri%20Lanka.pdf

Gorgonio, T. and Miller, A. (2005) 'Need To Know List', Oxfam GB Philippines and Oxfam GB (internal).

The HAP Principles of Accountability, available at: http://www.hapinternational.org/en/page.php?ID page =3&IDcat=10

IFRC (1994) 'The Code of Conduct for the International Red Cross and Red Crescent Movement and NGOs in Disaster Relief', available at: http://www.ifrc.org/ publicat/conduct/index.asp?navid =09_08

Jacobs, A. (2005) 'Accountability to Beneficiaries: A Practical Checklist', Mango for Oxfam GB, available at: http://www.mango.org.uk/guide/files/draft-accountability-checklist-nov05.doc

Phoeuk, S. (2005) 'Practical Guidelines on Humanitarian Accountability', Oxfam GB Cambodia (internal).

Sphere (2004) 'Common Standard 1: Participation', in *Sphere Humanitarian Charter and Minimum Standards in Disaster Response*, Sphere Project, available at: http://www.sphereproject.org/content/view/29/84/lang,English/

Wall, I. with UN-OCHA (2005) '"Where's My House?" : Improving communication with beneficiaries: an analysis of information flow to tsunami affected populations in Aceh Province', UNDP, available at: http://www.humanitarianinfo.org/sumatra/reference/assessments/doc/other/UNDP-WhereMyHouseFinal.pdf

Further information

Blagescu, M., de Las Casas, L., and Lloyd, R. (2005) 'Pathways to Accountability: A Short Guide to the Global Accountability Project Framework', One World Trust, available at: http:/www.oneworldtrust.org/pages/download.cfm?did=315

Cabassi, J. (2004) 'Involvement of PLHA (People living with HIV/AIDS)', in *Renewing Our Voice: Code of Good Practice for NGOs Responding to HIV/AIDS*, the NGO HIV/AIDS Code of Practice Project, available at: http://www.ifrc.org/Docs/pubs/health/hivaids/NGOCode.pdf?health/hivaids/NGOCode.pdf

HAP International (forthcoming, 2007) 'Manual of Humanitarian Accountability and Quality Management'.

UNHCR (2006) 'A rights-based approach including accountability to refugees', in *Operational Protection in Camps and Settlements*, available at: http://www.unhcr.org/publ/PUBL/448d6c122.pdf

Profile the people affected by the emergency (Section 2)

Sources

Burns, S. and Cupitt, S. (2003) 'Managing outcomes: a guide for homelessness organisations', Charities Evaluation Services, available at: http://www.ces-vol.org.uk/downloads/managingoutcomes-16-22.pdf

Clifton, D. (2004) 'Gender Standards for Humanitarian Responses', Oxfam GB (internal).

Feuerstein, M.-T. (1986) *Partners in Evaluation: Evaluating Development and Community Programmes with Participants*, Macmillan (adapted), available from: http://www.talcuk.org/catalog/product_info.php?manufacturers_id=&products_id=225&osCsid=ed7945aaa4079bfe51af4fb2413c4cc6. To order copies in bulk please contact Victoria Rose at Macmillan Education: vrose@macmillan.com

Gosling, L. with Edwards, M. (2003) *Toolkits: a practical guide to planning, monitoring, evaluation and impact measurement*, Save the Children, available from: http://www.savethechildren.org.uk/scuk/jsp/resources/details.jsp?id=594&group=resources&section=publication&subsection=details

Groupe Urgence Réhabilitation Développement for ALNAP (2003) *Participation by Crisis-Affected Populations in Humanitarian Action: A Handbook for Practitioners*, draft, available at: http://www.alnap.org/publications/gs_handbook/gs_handbook.pdf

IFRC (2005) *World Disasters Report 2005*, available at: http://www.ifrc.org/publicat/wdr2005/index.asp

IFRC (2000) 'Disaster Emergency Needs Assessment', in *Disaster Preparedness Training Manual*, available at: http://www.ifrc.org/cgi/pdf_dp.pl?disemnas.pdf

Oxfam (no date) 'Background Information: Checklist for Rapid Assessments In Emergencies', (internal).

Schofield, R. (2003) 'Do's of interviewing beneficiaries', Medair (internal).

Sphere (2004) 'Common Standard 2: Initial Assessment', in *Sphere Humanitarian Charter and Minimum Standards in Disaster Response*, Sphere Project, available at: http://www.sphereproject.org/content/view /30/84/lang,English/

Srodecki, J. (2001) 'World Vision Use of Sphere Standards in a Large Scale Emergency: A Case Study of the Spring 2001 Gujarat Response', World Vision International (internal).

USAID Centre for Development Information and Evaluation (1996) 'Conducting Focus Group Interviews', in *Performance Monitoring and Evaluation TIPS*, number 10, available at: http://www.usaid.gov/ pubs/usaid_eval/ascii/pnaby233.txt

Walden, V. M. (no date), 'Focus group discussion', Oxfam GB (internal).

World Vision (no date) 'Rapid child protection assessment form in situations of natural disasters', (internal).

Further information

Cabassi, J. (2004) 'Involvement of PLHA (People living with HIV/AIDS)', in *Renewing Our Voice: Code of Good Practice for NGOs Responding to HIV/AIDS*, the NGO HIV/AIDS Code of Practice Project, available at: http://www.ifrc.org/Docs/pubs/health/hivaids/ NGOCode.pdf?health/hivaids/NGOCode.pdf

Inter-agency Standing Committee (2006) *Women, Girls, Boys and Men: Different Needs – Equal Opportunities: A Gender Handbook for Humanitarian Action*, (draft), available at: http://www.humanitarian info.org/iasc/content/documents/default.asp?docID= 1948&publish=0

Inter-agency Standing Committee (2005) *Guidelines for Gender-Based Violence Interventions in Humanitarian Settings (Arabic, English, French, Bahasa Indonesia or Spanish)*, available at: http://www.humanitarianinfo. org/iasc/content/subsidi/tf_gender/gbv.asp

Jones, H. and Reed, B. (2005) *Water and Sanitation for Disabled People and Other Vulnerable Groups: Designing services to improve accessibility*, WEDC, available at: http://wedc.lboro.ac.uk/publications/details.php? book=1%2084380%20079%209

'Keeping Children Safe: Standards for Child Protection', available at: http://www.keepingchildrensafe.org.uk

Mobility International USA (2004) 'Checklist for inclusion', available at: http://www.miusa.org/pub-lications/freeresources/Checklist_for_Inclusion.pdf

Office of the United Nations High Commissioner for Refugees (2006) 'UNHCR Tool for Participatory Assessment in Operation', available at: http://www.unhcr.org/publ/PUBL/450e963f2.html

Slim, H. and Bonwick, A. (2006) *Protection: an ALNAP Guide for Humanitarian Agencies*, Oxfam, available at: http://www.odi.org.uk/alnap/publications/protection/ alnap_protection_guide.pdf

USAID (2005) *Field Operations Guide for Disaster Assessment and Response: Version 4.0*, available at: http://www.usaid.gov/our_work/humanitarian_assistance/disaster_assistance/resources/pdf/fog_v3.pdf

Wells, J. (2005) 'Checklist for older persons in internally displaced persons camps' in 'Protecting and assisting older people in emergencies', HPN Network Paper 53, Overseas Development Institute, available at: http://www.odihpn.org/report.asp?ID=2758

Identify the changes people want to see (Section 3)

Sources

Bishop, L. (2002) 'First steps in Monitoring and Evaluation', Charities Evaluation Services, available at: http://www.ces-vol.org.uk/downloads/first-mande-15-21.pdf

Centre for Participation, NEF (2001) 'Prove it!', New Economics Foundation, available at: http://www.neweconomics.org/gen/z_sys_publicationdetail.aspx?pid=52

Clark, Margarita, Save the Children, interview.

Clarke, Nigel, interview.

Gosling, L. with Edwards, M. (2003) *Toolkits: a practical guide to planning, monitoring, evaluation and impact measurement*, Save the Children, available from: http://www.savethechildren.org.uk/scuk/jsp/resources/details.jsp?id=594&group=resources&section=publication&subsection=details

Oxfam GB (no date) 'Rebuilding Lives in Sri Lanka for Tsunami Affected People: Oxfam's Integrated Transitional Shelter Programme'.

Sphere (2004) 'Scope and limitations of the Sphere handbook', in *Sphere Humanitarian Charter and Minimum Standards in Disaster Response*, Sphere Project, available at: http://www.sphereproject.org/content/view/23/84/lang,English/

Walden, V. M. (2005) 'Community Indicators', Oxfam (internal).

Further information

Jobes, K. (1997) 'Participatory Monitoring and Evaluation Guidelines, Experiences in the field, St Vincent and the Grenadines', DFID, available at: http://portals.wi.wur.nl/files/docs/ppme/PPME.pdf

Sigsgaard, P. (2002) 'Monitoring without indicators', *Evaluation Journal of Australasia* 2 (1), available at: http://www.aes.asn.au/publications/Vol2No1/monitoring_without_indicators_msc.pdf

Sphere (2004) 'Common Standard 3: Response', in *Sphere Humanitarian Charter and Minimum Standards in Disaster Response*, Sphere Project, available at: http://www.sphereproject.org/content/view/31/84/lang,English/

Sphere (2004) 'Common Standard 4: Targeting', in *Sphere Humanitarian Charter and Minimum Standards in Disaster Response*, Sphere Project, available at: http://www.sphereproject.org/content/view/32/84/lang,English/

Track changes and make feedback a two-way process (Section 4)

Sources

Burns, S. and Cupitt, S. (2003) 'Managing outcomes: a guide for homelessness organisations', Charities Evaluation Services, available at: http://www.ces-vol.org.uk/downloads/managingoutcomes-16-22.pdf

Danish Refugee Council and HAP International (2006) 'Complaints-handling for the Humanitarian Sector: Seminar Report', available at: http://www.hap international.org/en/complement.php?IDcomplement =57&IDcat=4&IDpage=76

Feuerstein, M.-T. (1986) *Partners in Evaluation: Evaluating Development and Community Programmes with Participants*, Macmillan (adapted), available from: http://www.talcuk.org/catalog/product_info. php?manufacturers_id=&products_id=225&osCsid= ed7945aaa4079bfe51af4fb2413c4cc6. To order copies in bulk please contact Victoria Rose at Macmillan Education: vrose@macmillan.com

Meissner R., Zachariah, A., and Schofield, R. (2005) 'Beneficiary feedback tools in West Darfur', *HAP International Newsletter 5*, August, available at: http://www.hapinternational.org/pdf_word/887-Newsletter%20Issue%20no%205.doc

Schofield, R. and Primrose, J., Medair, written communication.

Walden, V. M. (2005) 'Monitoring and Evaluation', Oxfam (internal).

Watt, John, interview.

Wilson, Pauline, written communication.

Further information

CDA Collaborative Learning Projects (2005) 'Report of The Listening Project, Aceh, Indonesia', November, available at: http://www.cdainc.com

International Council of Voluntary Agencies (2006) 'Building Safer Organisations project: resources on protection from sexual exploitation and abuse', available at: http://www.icva.ch/doc00000706.html

Mango (2005) 'Who Counts? Financial Reporting to Beneficiaries: Why is it Important?', available at: http://www.mango.org.uk/guide/files/who-counts-why-it-is-important-apr05.doc

People In Aid (2003) 'People In Aid Code of Good Practice in the Management and Support of Aid Personnel', available at: http://www.peopleinaid.org/code/online.aspx

Sphere (2004) 'Common Standard 5: Monitoring', in *Sphere Humanitarian Charter and Minimum Standards in Disaster Response*, Sphere Project, available at: http://www.sphereproject.org/content/view/33/84/lang,English/

Sphere (2004) 'Common Standard 6: Evaluation', in *Sphere Humanitarian Charter and Minimum Standards in Disaster Response*, Sphere Project, available at: http://www.sphereproject.org/content/view/34/84/lang,English/

Use feedback to improve project impact (Section 5)

Sources

Gorgonio, T. (2006) 'Notes on Accountable Exit from Communities when Programmes Close', Oxfam GB Philippines (internal).

Miller, Auriol, interview

Owubah, C., Greenblott, K. , and Zwier, J. (2005) 'Top 10 C-SAFE Initiatives in Monitoring & Evaluation', CARE, CRS, World Vision, ADRA, USAID, available at: http://pdf.dec.org/pdf_docs/PNADE672.pdf

Further information

'Key Messages from ALNAP's Review of Humanitarian Action in 2003: Enhancing Learning at Field Level and Evaluating Humanitarian Action', available at: http://www.alnap.org/publications/RHA2003/pdfs/RHA03_KMS.pdf

Prasad, R. R. (2006) 'Sri Lanka, Giving voice to people's grievance', ReliefWeb, 21 June, available at: http://www.reliefweb.int/rw/rwb.nsf/db900SID/ACIO-6QYDWJ?OpenDocument

Roche, C., Kasynathan, N. , and Gowthaman, P. (2005) 'Bottom-up Accountability and the Tsunami', paper prepared for the International Conference on Engaging Communities, Oxfam Australia, Brisbane, 14–17 August, available at: http://www.engaging communities2005.org/abstracts/Roche-Chris-final.pdf

Abbreviations

ALNAP	The Active Learning Network for Accountability and Performance in Humanitarian Action
C-SAFE	Consortium for Southern Africa Food Security Emergency
ECB	The Emergency Capacity Building Project
HAP	Humanitarian Accountability Partnership International
NGO	Non-governmental organisation

Thank you

The Good Enough Guide was developed through wide-ranging consultation which began in November 2005. Input was through workshops and field tests and by face-to-face, e-mail, and phone discussion. The Emergency Capacity Building Project gratefully acknowledges the many organisations and individuals who contributed their expertise.

Project host

World Vision International

Editorial Committee

Sheryl Haw
Ivan Scott
Guy Sharrock
Julian Srodecki
Pauline Wilson

Project staff

Project Manager: Pauline Wilson
Knowledge Management and Research Officer:
Malaika Wright
Administration and Co-ordination: Susan Lee,
Sarah Gerein
ECB Project Director: Greg Brady

Consultants

Author : Sara Davidson
Field test leader: Christophe Lanord
Workshop leaders: Emma Jowett, Sean Lowrie,
Juan Sáenz, Ana Urgoiti

Contributors

Odette Abascal, Zonia Aguilar. Roberto Álvarez, Barbara Ammrati, Ribka Amsalu, Penny Anderson, Hugh Aprile, Jock Baker, Olga Bornemisza, Catalina Buciu, Maribel Carrera, Saskia Carusi, Esteban Casado, Mario Chang, Zia Choudhury, Margarita Clark, Nigel Clarke, Carlos Consuegra, Larry Dersham, Assane Diouf, Jagannath K. Dutta, Velida Dzino, Charlie Ehle, Francisco Enríquez, Hani Eskandar, Andy Featherstone, Mark Ferdig, Dane Fredenburg, Pamela Garrido, Meri Ghorkhmazyan, Juan Manuel Girón, Kent Glenzer, Krishnaswamy Gopalan, Ting Gorgonio, Marianna Hensley, Maurice Herson, Amy Hilleboe, Claudia Hoechst, Holly Inurretta, Iraida Izaguirre, Mark Janz, Alison Joyner, Nfanda Lamba, Liz Larson, Caroline Loftus, Richard Luff, Florame S. Magalong, Paul Majarowitz, Thabani Maphosa, Elisa Martinez, Daryl Martyris, Ayman Mashni, Cherian Mathew, Auriol Miller, Amilcar Miron, Eleanor Monbiot, Otilia Judith Mulul, Mayra Muralles, Mamadou Ndiaye , Monica Oliver, Danadevi Paz, Marion O'Reilly, Oxfam Aceh team, Chris Palusky, Warner Passanisi, Joshua Pepall, Sok Phoeuk, Adán Pocasangre, Maura Quinilla, Adhong Ramadhan, Lynn Renken, Claudia Reyna, Karen Robinson, Blaise Rodriguez, Mónica Rodríguez, Luis A. Rohr, Susan Romanski, Jim Rugh, Lauren Sable, Abdoulaye Sagne, Marco Vinicio Salazar, Robert Schofield, La Rue Seims, Daniel Selener, Gretchen Shanks, Juan Skinner, Aaron Skrocki, Clare Smith, Ingvild Solvang, Megan Steinke, Nicholas Stockton, Beatrice Teya, Ibrahima Thiandoum, Jutta Teigeler , Cristóbal Ventura, María E. Vidaurre, Carol Toms , Vivien Margaret Walden, Caroline Wegner, John Watt, Kelly Williams, A. Judi Wirjawan, Sharon Wilkinson , Ton van Zutphen

For your notes